# Contents

African Fish Eagle
*Haliaeetus vocifer*

Lion
*Panthera leo*
(page 14)

# THE MARA TRIANGLE

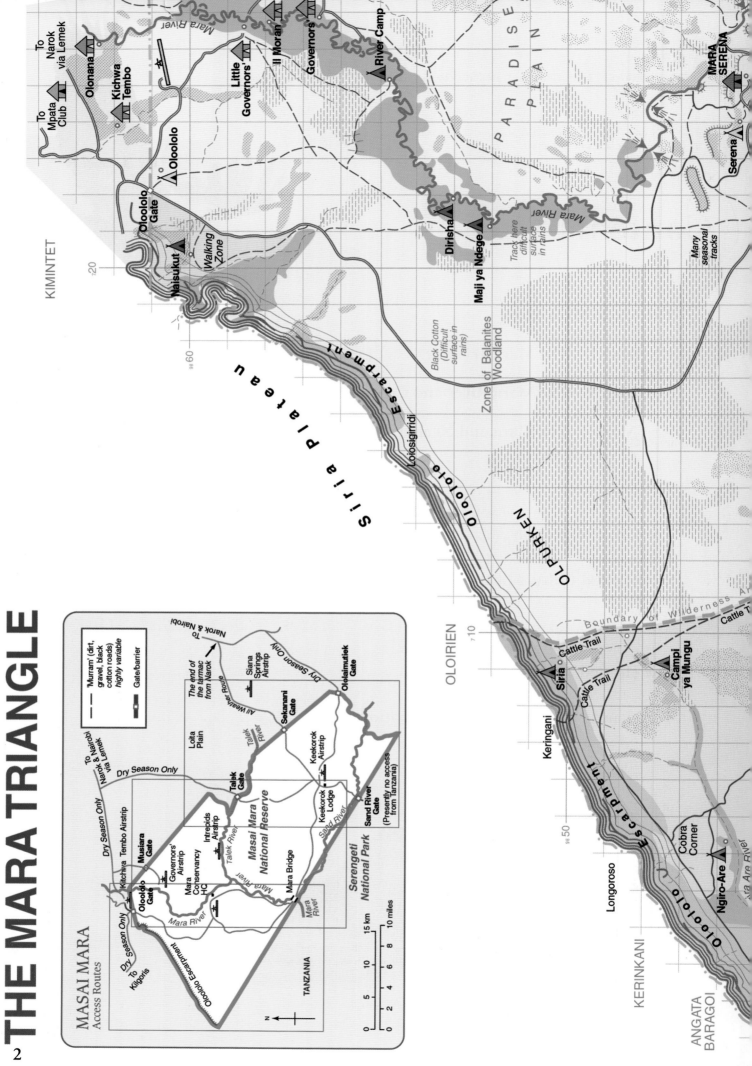

KIMINTET

Olonana

To Narok via Lemek

To Mpata Club

Kichwa Tembo

Oloololo

Oloololo Gate

Naisukut

Walking Zone

Little Governors'

Il Moran

Governors'

River Camp

PARADISE PLAIN

MARA SERENA

Serena

Mara River

Dirisha

Maji ya Ndege

Loiosigirridi

Siria Plateau

Oloololo Escarpment

Black Cotton (Difficult surface in rains)

Zone of Balanites Woodland

Track here difficult surface in rains

Mara River

Many seasonal tracks

OLPURKEN

Boundary of Wilderness Area

Cattle Trail

OLOIRIEN

Siria

Keringani

Cattle Trail

Cattle Trail

Campi ya Mungu

Longoroso

Escarpment

Cobra Corner

Ngiro-Are

Oloololo

KERINKANI

ANGATA BARAGOI

## MASAI MARA
### Access Routes

'Murram' (dirt, gravel, black cotton roads) highly variable

Gate/barrier

To Narok & Nairobi

The end of the tarmac from Narok

Loita Plain

All Weather River Route

Siana Springs Airstrip

Dry Season Only

Sekanani Gate

Talek River

Talek Gate

Keekorok Airstrip

Olelaimutiek Gate

Keekorok Lodge

Masai Mara National Reserve

To Nairobi Narok via Lemek

Dry Season Only

Kitchwa Tembo Airstrip

Musiara Gate

Governors' Airstrip

Intrepids Airstrip

Oloololo Gate

Mara Conservancy HC

Mara River

Talek River

Mara Bridge

Sand River

Sand River Gate
(Presently no access from Tanzania)

Serengeti National Park

Mara River

Dry Season Only

To Kilgoris

Oloololo Escarpment

TANZANIA

N

0   5   10   15 km

0   2   4   6   8   10 miles

2

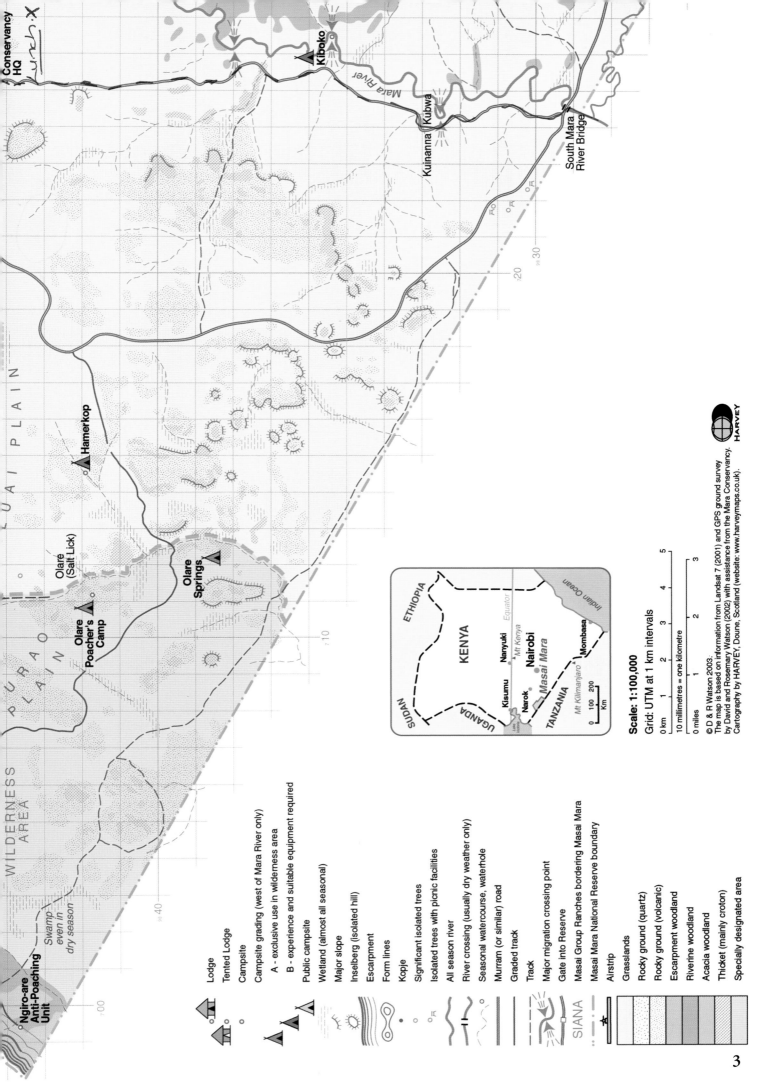

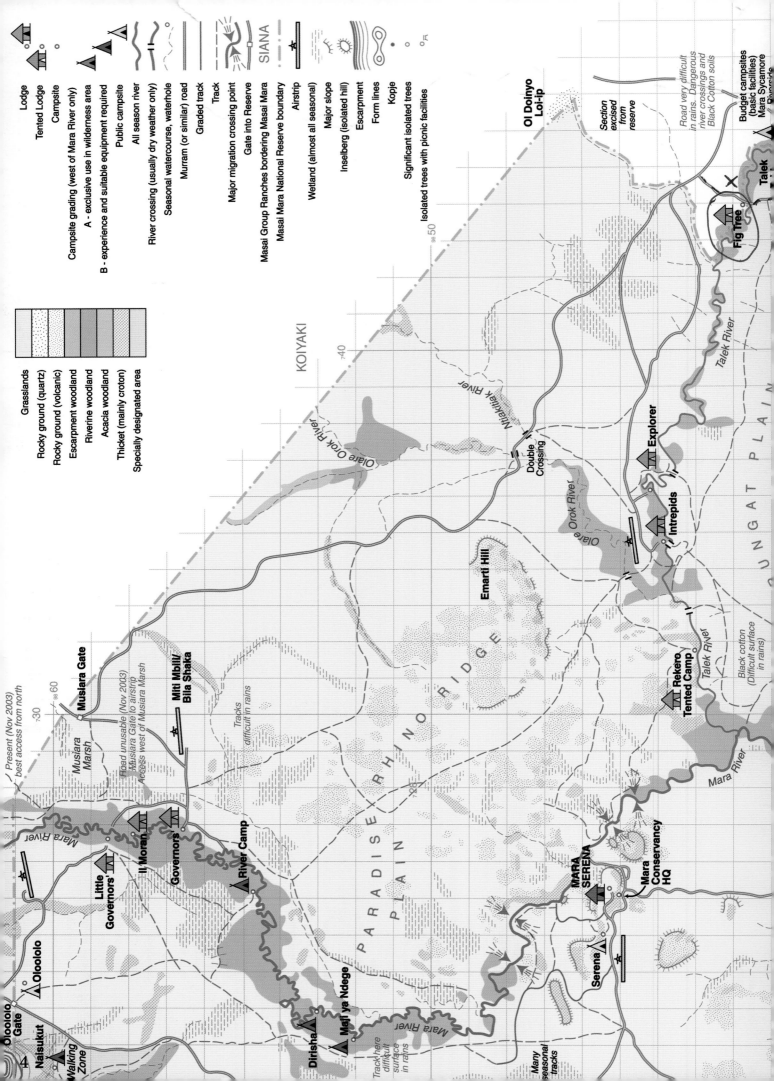

## Legend

**Grasslands**
**Rocky ground (quartz)**
**Rocky ground (volcanic)**
**Escarpment woodland**
**Riverine woodland**
**Acacia woodland**
**Thicket (mainly croton)**
**Specially designated area**

Lodge
Tented Lodge
Campsite
Campsite grading (west of Mara River only)
A - exclusive use in wilderness area
B - experience and suitable equipment required
Public campsite
All season river
River crossing (usually dry weather only)
Seasonal watercourse, waterhole
Murram (or similar) road
Graded track
Track
Major migration crossing point
Gate into Reserve
Masai Group Ranches bordering Masai Mara
Masai Mara National Reserve boundary
Airstrip
Wetland (almost all seasonal)
Major slope
Inselberg (isolated hill)
Escarpment
Form lines
Kopje
Significant isolated trees
Isolated trees with picnic facilities

SIANA

KOIYAKI

Ol Doinyo Loi-ip

*Section excised from reserve*

*Road very difficult in rains. Dangerous river crossings and Black Cotton soils*

Budget campsites (basic facilities)
Mara Sycamore

Talek

Fig Tree

Talek River

Olare Orok River

Ntiakitiak River

Double Crossing

Explorer

Intrepids

Olare Orok River

Emarti Hill

R H I N O   R I D G E

Rekero Tented Camp

Talek River

Black cotton (Difficult surface in rains)

Mara River

BUNGAT PLAIN

Musiara Gate

*Road unusable (Nov 2003) Musiara Gate to airstrip Access west of Musiara Marsh*

Miti Mbili/ Bila Shaka

Musiara Marsh

*Tracks difficult in rains*

'30

'98 60

*Present (Nov 2003) - best access from north*

Olololo Gate

Naisukut

Oloololo

*Walking Zone*

Mara River

Little Governors'

Il Moran

Governors'

River Camp

Dirisha

Maji ya Ndege

*Track here difficult surface in rains*

P A R A D I S E   P L A I N

Mara River

MARA SERENA

Mara Conservancy HQ

Serena

*Many seasonal tracks*

'40

98

'98

50

4

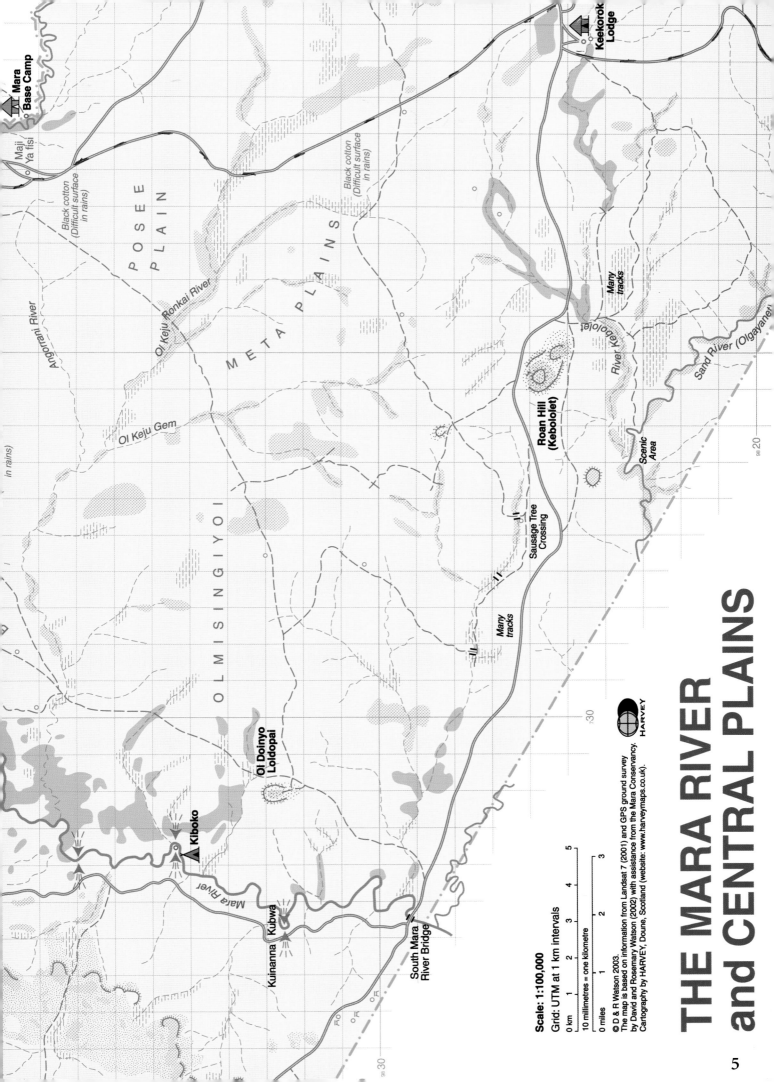

# THE MARA RIVER
# and CENTRAL PLAINS

**Mara Base Camp**

Maji Ya fisi

Black cotton
(Difficult surface
in rains)

Black cotton
(Difficult surface
in rains)

*in rains)*

Keekorok Lodge

P O S E E
P L A I N

M E T A   P L A I N S

Angorrani River

Ol Keju Ronkai River

Ol Keju Gem

O L M I S I N G I Y O I

*Many tracks*

River Kebololet

Sand River (Olgayanei)

*Scenic Area*

**Roan Hill (Kebololet)**

Sausage Tree Crossing

*Many tracks*

*Many tracks*

**Ol Doinyo Loldopai**

**Kiboko**

Mara River

Kuinanna Kubwa

**South Mara River Bridge**

**Scale: 1:100,000**
Grid: UTM at 1 km intervals

0 km   1   2   3   4   5

10 millimetres = one kilometre

0 miles   1   2   3

© D & R Watson 2003.
The map is based on information from Landsat 7 (2001) and GPS ground survey
by David and Rosemary Watson (2002) with assistance from the Mara Conservancy.
Cartography by HARVEY, Doune, Scotland (website: www.harveymaps.co.uk).

HARVEY

⁹⁸30

⁹⁸20

<sup>,</sup>30

5

# THE EASTERN MARA and NGAMA HILLS

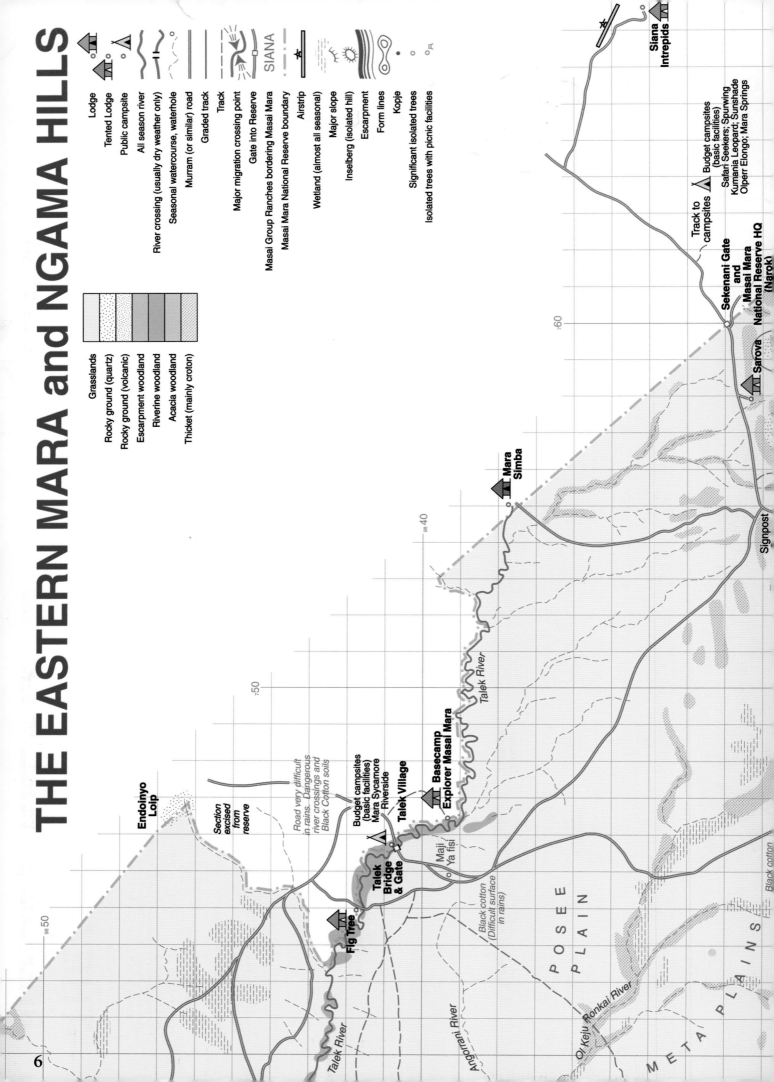

Legend:

- Lodge
- Tented Lodge
- Public campsite
- All season river
- River crossing (usually dry weather only)
- Seasonal watercourse, waterhole
- Murram (or similar) road
- Graded track
- Track
- Major migration crossing point
- Gate into Reserve
- Masai Group Ranches bordering Masai Mara
- Masai Mara National Reserve boundary
- Airstrip
- Wetland (almost all seasonal)
- Major slope
- Inselberg (isolated hill)
- Kopje
- Escarpment
- Form lines
- Significant isolated trees
- Isolated trees with picnic facilities

- Grasslands
- Rocky ground (quartz)
- Rocky ground (volcanic)
- Escarpment woodland
- Riverine woodland
- Acacia woodland
- Thicket (mainly croton)

SIANA

Siana Intrepids

Track to campsites

Budget campsites (basic facilities)

Safari Seekers; Spurwing
Kumania Leopard; Sunshade
Olperr Elongo; Mara Springs

Sekenani Gate and
Masai Mara National Reserve HQ (Narok)

Sarova

Signpost

Mara Simba

Talek River

Endoinyo Loip

*Section excised from reserve*

*Road very difficult in rains. Dangerous river crossings and Black Cotton soils*

Budget campsites (basic facilities)
Mara Sycamore Riverside

Basecamp
Explorer Masai Mara

Talek Village

Talek Bridge & Gate

Maji Ya fisi

Fig Tree

POSEE PLAIN

*Black cotton (Difficult surface in rains)*

Black cotton

Angorrani River

Talek River

Ol Keju Ronkai River

M E T A   P L A I N S

6

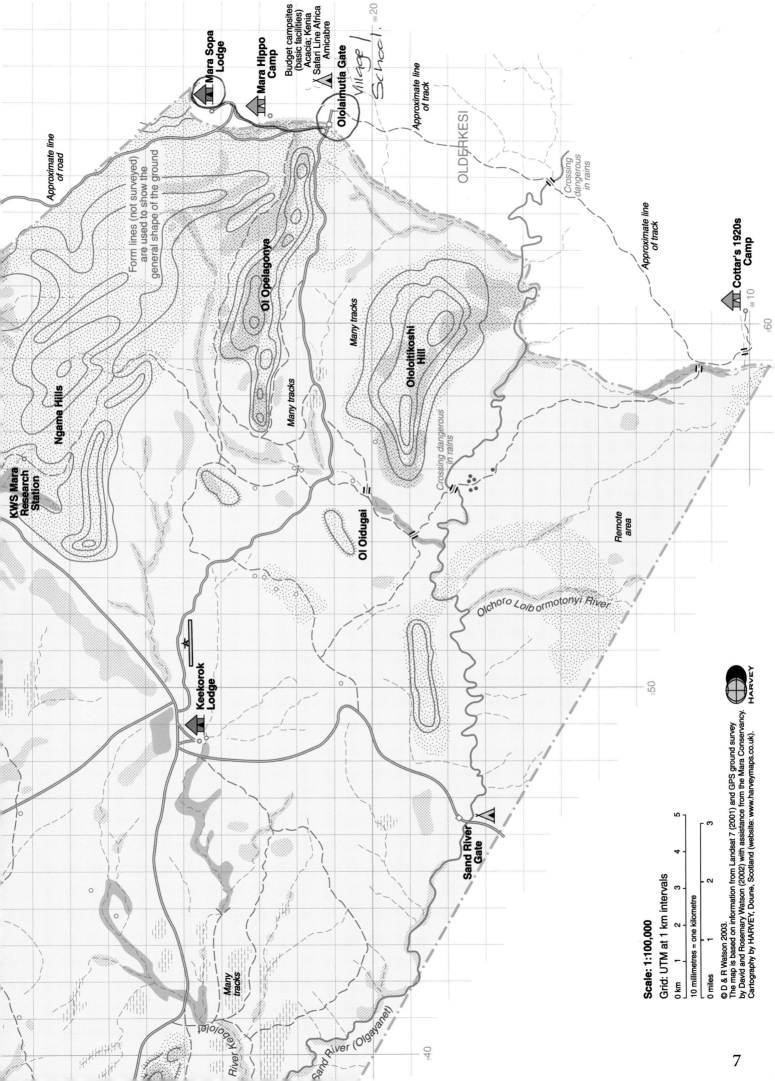

Mara Sopa Lodge

Mara Hippo Camp

Budget campsites (basic facilities)
Acacia; Kenia
Safari Line Africa
Amicabre

Ololaimutia Gate

Village / School 98 20

OLDERKESI

Approximate line of road

Approximate line of track

Approximate line of track

Crossing dangerous in rains

Cottar's 1920s Camp

98 10

Form lines (not surveyed) are used to show the general shape of the ground

Ol Opelagonya

Many tracks

Many tracks

Many tracks

Ololoitikoshi Hill

Crossing dangerous in rains

Ngama Hills

KWS Mara Research Station

Ol Oidugai

Remote area

Olchoro Loibormotonyi River

Keekorok Lodge

Many tracks

River Kaboloie (Olgayanet)

Sand River (Olgayanet)

Sand River Gate

98 40

98 50

98 60

**Scale: 1:100,000**

Grid: UTM at 1 km intervals

0 km   1   2   3   4   5

10 millimetres = one kilometre

0 miles   1   2   3

© D & R Watson 2003.
The map is based on information from Landsat 7 (2001) and GPS ground survey
by David and Rosemary Watson (2002) with assistance from the Mara Conservancy.
Cartography by HARVEY, Doune, Scotland (website: www.harveymaps.co.uk).

HARVEY

7

# The Ecozones

Ecozones are homes or habitats resulting from a collection of natural inputs. Species in a zone may be residents or migrants. The inputs include things like the altitude, the rocks and soil, and the climate, especially availability of water. All are inter-related, with each affecting the other. A little time understanding the different zones will much improve your visitor experience.

The diagram at the bottom shows a slice through the Masai Mara, west (left) to east (right). It shows rocks, soil and vegetation.

For example, the Oloololo Escarpment is a fault line along the edge of a massive intrusion or injection of hard granite; the Mara River flows over river alluvium and has steep earth banks; the Triangle uplands are volcanic, whereas the uplands of the east are made of quartz. On various kinds of rocks there is often a poorly drained clay called Black Cotton, which causes swamps and seasonally impassable roads. In addition, over the last fifty years or so, a combination of "fire" and "elephants" has caused the continuing change from a landscape of woodland and thicket to one now principally of grassland. The vegetation and the animals respond to all these things, and so the Mara is a combination of a variety of habitats or "ecozones".

Cattle Egrets in a swamp near the Mara River

**The Wetlands** – mainly seasonal, with few permanent wetlands. Usually occur where Black Cotton soil traps water at the surface, or underground streams re-emerge. Wetlands have lush, green vegetation, even in the dry season, and sometimes permanent water as at Musiara.
**Species:** buffalo, wildebeest, zebra, elephant, all predators, especially lion.

Mixed grasslands next to escarpment

**The Grasslands** – found on any type of rocks and increasing annually, as fire and elephant encroachment destroy the thickets. Red Oat Grass and Thatch Grass dominate. The landscape has classical rolling plains, with scattered trees such as in the Balanites savannah.
**Species:** enormous herds of grazers, especially wildebeest, zebra, gazelle; also topi, kongoni, eland, lion, cheetah, hyaena, jackal.

**The Oloololo Escarpment** – a continuous 400m, 45° slope along a fault line in the west, visible from almost everywhere in the Mara. Beyond, a gentle slope runs down to Lake Victoria, originally wooded, but, except in deep gullies, now mainly grass.
**Species:** most grazing animals, elephants, hyrax, leopard, klipspringer.

Rock Hyrax
*Procavia capensis*

Elephants with Oloololo Escarpment in the background

## Cross-section through the Masai Mara

**Plateau**
Ancient, hard Kilgoris granite; dipping gently west towards Lake Victoria.

Occupied by Maasai group ranches; scattered bush & grazing for cattle, sheep & goats.

**Escarpment**
Oloololo or Siria Escarpment 45°- 400m slope; streams disappear into lava at base.

Original trees now only in gullies & on some streams; otherwise grazing; often subject to annual burning.

**The Mara Triangle**
Phonolite lavas covering ancient Basement rocks; in places there are flat-topped low hills or 'inselbergs' with rocky outcrops & occasional swamps in between; plains are often covered in poorly drained Black Cotton soils; low areas west & north of Serena are swamp in rains, but fairly dry in between.

Mara Triangle is generally lush grazing, especially the seasonally flooded Black Cotton soils areas; shorter grass on exposed lavas; Croton & Euclea thickets on inselberg summits.

**The Mara River**
Stony, volcanic outcrops & difficult, rock-strewn terrain; Mara River alluvium produce rich soils; it is deeply incised between earth banks, making it difficult sometimes for migrating animals to leave the river.

Naturally Riverine Woodland, but fire & elephant-browsing now restrict this to north of the confluence of Mara & Talek rivers.

Granite

Black Cotton soil

Lava

Swamp

Rocky areas

Mara River & alluvium

Basement Rock

**The Riverine Forests –** the only Ecozone with continuous stands of tall trees; originally extensive; now mainly confined to the banks of Mara and Talek rivers, because of fire and encroachment by elephants. Tree species: *Warburgia ugandensis, Dyospyros abyssinica*, Phoenix Palm and Yellow-barked Acacia (Fever Tree).
**Species:** elephant, buffalo, bushbuck, waterbuck, duiker, hyrax, several monkey species and hundreds of birds.

Giraffe and zebra seeking shade on edge of Mara River forest

**The Triangle "inselbergs" –** meaning "island mountain". In the southern Triangle, there are a dozen or so quite spectacular low, flat-topped volcanic inselbergs, causing distinctive scenery, usually capped with Croton thicket. The rocks are distinctive, full of holes created by volcanic gases.
**Species:** impala, dik-dik, buffalo, lion.

Inselberg Knolls with thicket on summits

**The Mara River –** meanders between steep banks of alluvium, often 6m high, causing havoc to wildebeest and zebra during migration river crossings. Intermittent bands of resistant rock result in alternating rapids and scores of deep hippo pools. Hundreds of huge crocodiles lie in wait in the river. During migrations 2 million animals repeatedly run the gauntlet of this crossing.

Mara River crossing-point north of Serena

**The Thickets east of the Mara River –** on various sizes of quartz hills there are the largest remaining thickets in the Masai Mara. Soils are sandy and poor; hills may be covered in loose rock or scree. Annual fires thin out the Croton. But, after burning, the grasses between the bushes will be short and nutritious.
**Species:** rhino, warthog, dik-dik, impala, buffalo, eland and their predators.

Roan Hill thicket

**The Talek and Sand rivers–** seasonal rivers, sometimes a torrent, other times only a trickle or series of pools. The Sand River is sometimes spectacular, with lovely sandy "beaches". Many small streams have no obvious riverbed. Some are only evidenced in the dry season by a line of scattered Croton Bushes, reaching down to underground water.
**Species:** all grazers and predators.

Talek River near Rekero camp

**The Fig Trees and Sausage Trees –** shown as "significant isolated trees on the maps" and scattered throughout the Mara.
**Species:** elephant, wildebeest, impala and other animals use the shade; fruit and leaves are food for elephant, giraffe, monkeys, baboons.

Giant Sausage Tree

---

**The Central Plains**
Rolling plains on ancient rocks; sandy-brown soils; occasional Black Cotton soils with marshy patches during & after rains; isolated hills are usually outliers of quartz, though hills between Intrepids & Governors' are lava; streams are seasonal with rocky or sandy beds; rivers such as Talek are sometimes incised, whereas others are just shallow luggas (stream beds).

Plains are wide, open grasslands, interspersed with occasional thickets, especially in stream beds; woodland follows bigger rivers such as Talek, Sand & Olare Orok.

**The Eastern Hills**
Quartz hills, 100-200m above the general level of the plains; thin, sandy soils, often with stony slopes.

Mixed thickets; but much recent fire damage, even to the summits of hills; shrubs only partially recover.

Black Cotton soil

Black Cotton soil

Quartz

# The Great Migration

"Everyone who has a chance to see nearly two million animals on the move has been touched by the magic of this place. What is it that gets under our skin? The urgency of the movement of the wildebeest? The wide open plains? The African light? Or maybe it is the fact that we all came from here, not such a long time ago, and our deep unconsciousness remembers the time 6 000 generations ago… Or maybe it is just the sheer numbers of the migrating animals as they move in the world's last surviving great migration".

Markus Borner, Frankfurt Zoo representative in Serengeti, talking about the Great Migration.

## When did the World know?

It was in the late 1950s that father and son zoologists, Bernard and Michael Grzimek from Frankfurt Zoo first attempted to count the migrations of thousands of wildebeest, zebra and Thomson's Gazelle. They were the first to bring to the attention of the world the amazing Serengeti-Masai Mara eco-system around which we now see perhaps two million animals moving annually.

Wildebeest and zebra massing in the Mara grasslands

## What is the Pattern of Movement?

The wildebeest have their calves from December to May on the nutrient-rich grasses of the volcanic plains of the south-east Serengeti. As the plains begin to dry out, the animals start to migrate west, and then north towards the Masai Mara. The Mara is the best-watered area of the entire 25 000km² ecosystem, producing the lush Red Oat grasslands of the Mara Triangle west of the Mara River, and those of the central plains east of the river. The older, experienced animals lead the way, sensing water from up to 50km away.

## Is there a Social Structure in the Migration?

Apart from the relationship between mother and calf, wildebeest have no family ties. Moreover, there is no leader. Markus Borner tells us , *"Any individual can start walking, and tens of thousands might be following…If a lion or a crocodile eats the very temporary leader, the rest barely notice, the migration continues…"*

Lion flagging in the afternoon heat

## The Migration in the Masai Mara

The first lines of animals begin to appear in the Mara in June. Then, another herd comes from Loita, to the north-east. The exact nature of the movement is not understood. Classically it occurs in a clockwise swathe of migrating animals, with most coming into the Mara Triangle from the south-west. But some also come from the east and south-east, and are first seen east of Keekorok.

For the next four or five months they fill the grasslands of the Masai Mara, until the tall Red Oat Grass is reduced to a well-cropped lawn.

*Red-tip butterfly*

Spotted Hyaena resting with a full stomach

## The Predators on the Route

Even apart from the Mara River crossing, the life of the migrating animal is one of constant threat. The Masai Mara has the second highest lion density in the world, with over 500 lions in just over 1 500km². In addition thousands of animals are taken by other predators, including leopard and cheetah. Many are also eaten by hyaenas, who are serious hunters, and not just the scavengers they were once thought to be.

The number of predators is largely controlled by the population of indigenous, resident species such as buffalo and topi, that live permanently in their home range, and supply food for carnivores year-round.

## Crossing the Mara River

The Mara River bisects the Reserve, running from near the Oloololo Gate in the north-west, south to Mara Bridge. There is nothing more spectacular in nature than the crossing of the river by such enormous herds of migrating animals.

Sometimes thousands of animals will mass on the alluvial banks, 6 metres above the water, waiting for the opportune moment for a crossing. Below, waiting knowingly in the river, are the enormous Mara River crocodiles.

First one, then a few, and then a frenetic mass of animals leap into the water. At some places the banks are worn down after centuries of crossings; in other places they are vertical on both sides of the river. Animals plunge down the earth banks into the water, swim the 20 or 50 metres, depending on the chosen crossing point, and then struggle in their hundreds to find a safe way out on the other side. Here many will drown or succumb to crocodile attack. Thousands of animals cross safely, nearly 1.5 million in a "good" year. But thousands are also lost each year to crocodiles and to drowning.

Part of 1.3 million migrating wildebeest

## The Wildebeest leave the Mara

By the end of October, one can see lines of animals beginning a purposeful march to the south, heading home to Serengeti, and for the females to have their calves. The Red Oat Grass has been reduced to a yellow-brown stubble. Over four or five months, it is estimated that wildebeest alone will have deposited over 60 000 tons of dung in the Mara, to fertilise the grasslands for next year's migrations.

When the wandering zebra, wildebeest and Thomson's Gazelle have moved south for the year, they still leave behind one of Africa's largest concentrations of other plains animals – buffalo, topi, impala, kongoni and elephant, amongst many others, perhaps enjoying the fact that the visit of their southern cousins is over for another 6 or 7 months.

## The Future

The Maasai are not hunters, and the wildebeest and zebra pass through the Maasai lands without being molested. However, on the western fringes of the migration routes, there is a culture of hunting for game meat. Current estimates suggest perhaps 40 000 animals are taken annually by poachers. Markus Borner believes this a sustainable number. But if the number poached were to double, the wildebeest population would crash.

**Will this paradise continue? Will a sustainable balance be achieved which is fair to both animals and humans? It would be sad to think that we are the last generation who will witness this final, amazing demonstration of this wonder of nature, the Great Migration.**

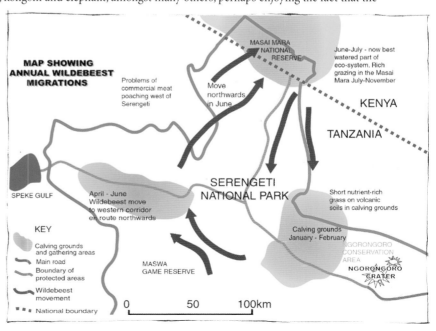

**MAP SHOWING ANNUAL WILDEBEEST MIGRATIONS**

Problems of commercial meat poaching west of Serengeti

Move northwards in June

June-July - now best watered part of eco-system. Rich grazing in the Masai Mara July-November

KENYA

TANZANIA

SPEKE GULF

April - June Wildebeest move to western corridor en route northwards

SERENGETI NATIONAL PARK

Short nutrient-rich grass on volcanic soils in calving grounds

Calving grounds January - February

NGORONGORO CONSERVATION AREA

NGORONGORO CRATER

MASWA GAME RESERVE

**KEY**

Calving grounds and gathering areas

Main road

Boundary of protected areas

Wildebeest movement

National boundary

0    50    100km

# The Maasai and the Formation of The National Reserve

The Maasai came from their original homeland of southern Sudan in the Nile Valley. They began to migrate south and east about 500 years ago, with a group called the Nilo-Hamitics, that included groups like the Maasai, the Samburu, Pokot and others. The Maasai are a linguistic group, being identified by their common language "Maa". Oral tradition says they arrived in the area of the Mara around the end of the 17th Century to the start of the 18th. So they have been here for about 300 years.

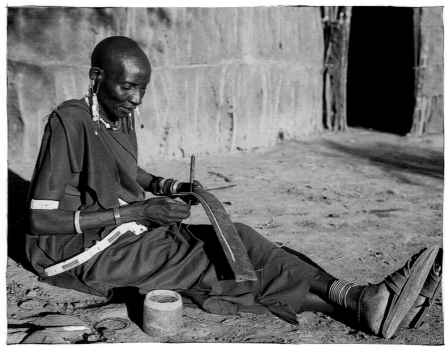

Maasai woman beading a belt

## Who are the Maasai?

Though not the most powerful tribe politically in East Africa, the Maasai are certainly the best known. They are recognised for their handsome appearance, and also for being brave, stubborn, sometimes arrogant, and fiercely proud of their culture and traditions. They are clearly identifiable – the men wearing their bright red cloaks, often carrying a spear and *rungu* (short club); the women colourfully dressed and festooned in bangles and beads. In spite of modern education, many Maasai still follow traditional age-group ceremonies and rituals, many men going through the three stages of boyhood, warrior and elder.

## The Maasai in Kenya's History

When the British and German colonialists arrived in Kenya at the end of the 19th Century, the Maasai people occupied an area from central Tanzania to Mount Kenya. Since then, they have seen their lands dissected by national boundaries and by the expansion of other groups.

European colonisation brought with it death and disease – in the 1880s and 1890s, rinderpest almost wiped out the Maasai cattle and related wildlife such as buffalo and wildebeest. The people similarly were seriously affected by diseases such as smallpox and cholera. At the start of the 20th Century, the Maasai people were in a sorry state, and it took another half century for both animals and people to recover. The health of the people improved as diseases were controlled, and eventually, when cattle were vaccinated, rinderpest was eradicated and domestic and wild animal populations rapidly began to recover. Although some animal numbers have declined (e.g. Rhino and the African Hunting Dog), present cattle numbers and most wildlife are probably at an all-time high.

Maasai men in their identifiable bright red robes at Sekanani Gate

## Cattle and the Maasai

Cattle are at the hub of Maasai existence. Homes are located around a cattle stockade, the *Enkang* (sometimes called the *Manyatta*). Cattle are the major sign of wealth and a medium of exchange. The products of cattle – milk, blood, hides and even dung (used in house building) – are all central to the way of life. Traditionally, unlike other tribes, the Maasai have never hunted wild animals for food, but depend on their cows, together with sheep and goats. Effectively they live at peace with wildlife.

With two long dry periods, the seasonal search for grazing provided the reason for the Maasai semi-nomadic way of life.

Traditionally open plains are now being fenced, and some Maasai lands (e.g. north of the Reserve beyond Lemek) are used for extensive wheat cultivation.

## The Maasai and the Mara

The word "Mara" means spotted or mottled in the Maasai language. Most of the names of places are descriptive. Another you will know is "Serengeti", meaning wide or seemingly never-ending plains.

Contrary to what you might expect, the Masai Mara is not a national park, like Tsavo or Amboseli, but is designated the Masai Mara National Reserve. In the middle of the last century, after the eradication of rinderpest, numbers of both cattle and wildlife began to expand, and in 1948 the Mara Triangle (see Map 1, pages 2 – 3), the western end of the present Reserve, and about 520km², became a National Game Reserve. In 1961, the protected area was extended east of the Mara River, and in 1984 various adjustments were made to create the Masai Mara National Reserve with its present boundaries, an area of just over 1 500km².

The Reserve is controlled by the Narok and Trans-Mara County Councils. In 2001 the management of the Triangle was ceded to the Mara Conservancy, a highly successful wildlife management experiment.

Family outside typical Maasai dwelling

Young Maasai women in full adornment

Decorative head- and neck-wear

Although you will occasionally see Maasai cattle encroaching into the Reserve, the Maasai now live around the protected area on three sides. Wild animals, however, recognise no man-made boundaries, and often there is as much wildlife outside the Reserve as in it.

The Maasai are divide into sub-tribes, of which there are four or five adjacent or close to the Mara. The land is organised within areas called "group ranches" – seven of these are immediately next to the Reserve. Distribution of a proportion of income from gate receipts, lodges etc is done via the group ranches.

When Maasai come to your lodge or camp to work, to dance or for cultural talks etc, they will generally be coming from the *Enkang* along the northern or western border of the Reserve.

## The Maasai and the future of the Masai Mara

The future of the Masai Mara depends on good, sustainable management which takes into account the needs both of the animals and also of the people.

It will make the most sense if the healthy survival of the Mara increasingly becomes the Maasai people's number one financial asset, where everyone can clearly see its benefits.

# The Hunters

Animal hunters have always fascinated us, perhaps because we were hunters too. The animals in Africa have lived among human and animal predators for millennia, and are well adapted to survive with them. Predators use different strategies to catch their prey.

## Lion and cheetah

During the migrations lions feed mainly on wildebeest and zebra. However, it is the number of resident species such as buffalo, topi, kongoni and impala which control lion populations. The Mara has over 500 lions, many in very large prides of occasionally over 30 individuals, with each pride occupying its own range.

Cheetah are among the most successful hunters, catching half of all animals they chase. They live on the open plains, where they can best make use of their speed to catch their prey. Females normally hunt and raise their cubs on their own. Males form sibling groups of 1 - 4 individuals, and often hunt together.

## Lion

*Panthera leo*: height: 1 m; mass: M: 180 - 230kg, F: 120 - 160kg; life expectancy: 13 - 15 years. Lions are social cats. They often hunt for larger prey, such as zebra, in groups of two or more, as this increases their success rate.

*Lioness skull*

Lions normally try to get as close as possible to their prey, before going in for the kill.

Lions stalk with their heads low, legs bent, and bodies tense and ready to react. They move only when the prey is not looking in their direction. When they are within 20 - 30 metres, they rush at the herd and try to scatter it in panic. The other lions in the hunt try to cut off one member of the herd.

*Prey - Plains Zebra (see page 20)*

The best-positioned lion surges forward and leaps onto the rump or shoulders of the chosen prey, throwing the animal off balance. As soon as it falls, it is grabbed by the throat to strangle or suffocate it. Sometimes it bleeds to death. The lions start feeding at the groin where the skin is soft, tearing it open to expose the intestines, which are eaten first. The strongest lions feed first, and they tear the skin over the back to expose the flesh of the limbs.

If the males hear the lionesses feeding, they rush in, pushing the females off the kill. Females, too, have their fill before allowing cubs to feed. If there is still meat left over after the first "banquet", the pride often stays around to guard it against scavengers.

# Cheetah

*Acinonyx jubatus*:
height: 75 - 80cm; mass: 40 - 50kg;
life expectancy: 10 - 15 years.
Cheetah can be identified by the
characteristic tearmarks, and by the
fact that their spots are solid, and
not arranged in rosettes like those
of the leopard.

*Cheetah are the only
cats without retractable
claws.*

Cheetah often rest on mounds and fallen trees,
from where they locate their prey, using
both eyes and ears.

Mara cheetahs prey
especially on Thomson's
Gazelle, and also on the
young of a variety of species
such as wildebeest, topi and
impala. They start rushing
at the prey from 70 - 100m away.
Cheetah can run at up to 112km/h,
averaging about 64km/h. They can
pursue their prey for about 300m.

The faster the fleeing animal
runs, the easier it is to
knock it off balance.

The cheetah brings down the
prey by striking the rump, thigh
or hind legs sideways or
downwards with a forepaw, or by
simply tripping it. The large
dewclaw on the cheetah's front
foot often helps to trip an
animal.

*Prey - Young impala*

*Scavenging Black-backed Jackal
(see page 18)*

The prey is grabbed from behind and strangled.
It is taken by the throat and dragged to cover before the
cheetah starts feeding. First the groin is torn open with
the cheek teeth, exposing the muscles of the limbs
and back. These and the neck muscles are
normally eaten first. If disturbed by other
predators, cheetah do not return to their kills.
Jackal seldom come within 30m of a
cheetah feeding as the cheetah's speed
makes it too dangerous for
the jackal to risk stealing
scraps.

15

# Leopard, serval and crocodile

Leopard and serval prefer the dense vegetation in riverine areas, where their spotted coats blend with the shadows. They are nocturnal hunters. The best times to find them are very early in the morning and late in the afternoon, or on night drives.

The crocodile is a very efficient killer. While waiting submerged in muddy water for better concealment, it resembles a log. Adults eat mostly fish, but also terrapins, birds and mammals.

## Leopard

*Panthera pardus*: height: 70cm; mass: 40 - 80kg; life expectancy: 15 years. Identify leopards by their spots arranged in black rosettes with a yellow-brown centre. Solitary predators, they are more successful when they hunt at night. Leopard often lie in wait in dry stream beds, or on well-used paths to waterholes, where they ambush animals that come by. The leopard waits until the prey is very close (about 3m), then pounces before it has time to react. To kill the prey, the leopard first paralyses it with a bite through the back of the neck that damages the spinal cord.

The leopard then strangles the prey with its powerful jaws. The kill is taken by the neck and dragged away between the leopard's legs. They are very strong, and can lift a carcass of their own weight into a tree.

*Lichen patches on bark help Leopard to blend into their environment*

Prey the size of a large impala can last for more than one meal. It is usually wedged tightly into a fork in a tree with dense foliage, about 6m above the ground. This protects it from scavengers and from other carnivores. Look for prey stored away from scavengers in trees, especially along river beds like the Talek.

Long hair is plucked from the carcass before the leopard feeds, and bits of hair can often be seen lying on the ground under a tree where it has stored a kill. It starts feeding at the back of the carcass, in the tender groin and anal region. Then it eats the hind-quarter where there is the most flesh. The stomach is left for the hyaenas, which often wait under the tree.

Leopard usually feed at night, and take 2 - 3 days to finish a carcass. After feeding and cleaning itself, it rests close by, where the unfinished carcass can be watched.

*Leopard skull*

*Prey - Impala female*

## Serval

*Felis serval:* height: 50cm;
mass: 8,5 - 13kg; life expectancy: 12 years
Serval hunt during the day, using their large ears and acute hearing to detect
the exact position of the prey, often rodents and frogs. Prey is caught in one or more pounces
that may span 1 - 4m, and can be up to 1 m high. Serval discard the gut before eating the rest
of the kill head first.

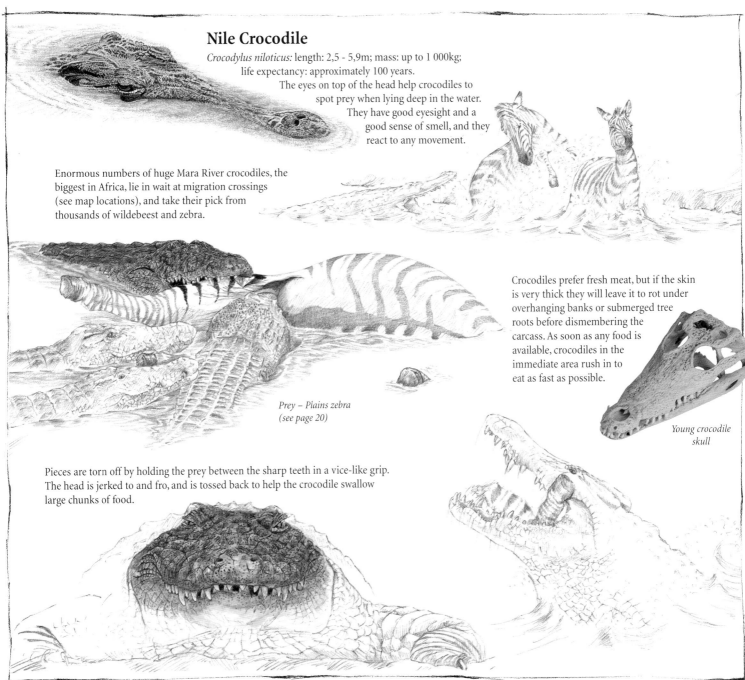

## Nile Crocodile

*Crocodylus niloticus:* length: 2,5 - 5,9m; mass: up to 1 000kg;
life expectancy: approximately 100 years.
The eyes on top of the head help crocodiles to
spot prey when lying deep in the water.
They have good eyesight and a
good sense of smell, and they
react to any movement.

Enormous numbers of huge Mara River crocodiles, the
biggest in Africa, lie in wait at migration crossings
(see map locations), and take their pick from
thousands of wildebeest and zebra.

Crocodiles prefer fresh meat, but if the skin
is very thick they will leave it to rot under
overhanging banks or submerged tree
roots before dismembering the
carcass. As soon as any food is
available, crocodiles in the
immediate area rush in to
eat as fast as possible.

*Prey – Plains zebra
(see page 20)*

*Young crocodile
skull*

Pieces are torn off by holding the prey between the sharp teeth in a vice-like grip.
The head is jerked to and fro, and is tossed back to help the crocodile swallow
large chunks of food.

# Hyaenas, jackals and vultures

Predators often do not eat all of their kill. They usually leave behind a carcass of bones, skin, innards and sometimes some flesh, which provide food for a vast range of other creatures. These range from insects like Blowflies and their maggots, to the larger, scavenging mammals and birds. They ensure that the carcass is totally cleaned or devoured, which helps to control dangerous diseases such as botulism and anthrax.

Of the larger scavengers that work together to clear carcasses, some have strong teeth or beaks to tear skin and break bones. These include hyaena and White-backed Vulture that move in, dominate, and eat as fast and as much as possible. Smaller animals such as Black-backed Jackals and Hooded Vultures rely on their speed to compete at a kill.

## Black-backed Jackal

*Canis mesomelas:*
height: 38cm; mass: 7 - 10kg; life expectancy: 13 years. Jackals are omnivorous hunters and scavengers, eating a wide variety of food including carrion, rodents, reptiles and birds. They hunt singly, by night or day, and react very fast, often catching birds coming down to drink. When hunting bigger prey, jackals work in pairs or larger groups.

*Dove feathers*

*Prey - Laughing Dove*

They often select weaker animals such as impala lambs or old, sick animals. As their prey is more visible in open areas, this is where jackals are often seen.

## Spotted Hyaena

*Crocuta crocuta:*
height: 70 - 85cm; mass: 65 - 70kg; life expectancy: 15 - 20 years. Hyaenas are very successful hunters, more than half their food consisting of their own kills. Newborn impalas are especially vulnerable, and make up a large proportion of the hyaena's diet. At other times, they scavenge, and hunt young, small animals. Hyaenas detect their prey by both smell and hearing. They lie up and wait for a young animal to move far enough away from its mother to make it easy prey.

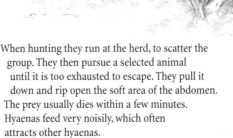

When hunting they run at the herd, to scatter the group. They then pursue a selected animal until it is too exhausted to escape. They pull it down and rip open the soft area of the abdomen. The prey usually dies within a few minutes. Hyaenas feed very noisily, which often attracts other hyaenas.

*Prey - Young impala*

Hyaena's jaws and teeth are well adapted to splintering and crushing bones, and shearing through sinew and hide. They digest bones, which is why their dung is characteristically white.

# Vultures

Vultures are often not first to a carcass, but are preceded by the sharp-sighted and ever-soaring Bateleur Eagle. Solitary White-headed Vultures are also among the first to locate a carcass. They are forced to give up feeding if large numbers of White-backed Vultures arrive. Pairs of neat, monk-like Hooded Vultures often arrive at the carcass after the Bateleurs and White-headed Vultures, but are often the first to feed. The largest of the southern African vultures, the unmistakable Lappet-faced Vulture, usually arrives last, and stands around on the outskirts. Because of its size it can chase the others away, and feeds mostly on tough skin and ligaments that the other vultures cannot manage.

The common Ruppell's Griffon Vulture relies on vision not scent to locate kills. With a relatively weak beak, it often waits for other vultures to open up the carcass. It can be seen in very large numbers feeding on the hundreds of carcasses in the Mara River during the migrations.

**▼ Bateleur**
*Terathopius ecaudatus*
length: 55 - 70cm;
mass: 1,8 - 2,9kg.

**▲ White-headed Vulture**
*Trigonoceps occipitalis*
length: 78 - 82cm;
mass: 3,3 - 5,3kg.

**Lappet-faced Vulture ►**
*Torgos tracheliotus*
length: 98 - 105cm; mass: 5,9 - 7,9kg.

**▲ Ruppell's Griffon Vulture**
*Gyps fulvus*
length: 97 - 107cm;
mass: 6 - 7kg.

*Carcass - Impala male*

**▲ Hooded Vulture**
*Necrosyrtes monachus*
length: 65 - 75cm;
mass: 1,8 - 2,6kg.

White-backed Vultures are gregarious birds that follow the smaller vultures and Bateleur to a carcass, chasing other scavenging birds away. A large group of White-backed Vultures can consume an impala in 10 minutes, unless they are chased off by a stronger animal.

Black-backed Jackal can chase off even White-backed Vultures, waiting for a chance to snatch a titbit.

**White-backed Vulture ►**
*Gyps africanus*
length: 90 - 98cm;
mass: 4,4 - 7,9kg.

*White-backed Vulture*

Hyaenas often arrive at the remains of a carcass before the vultures have a chance to feed. They eat as fast and as much as possible. There is often an ongoing battle for supremacy at the carcass between White-backed Vultures and hyaenas. Hyaenas usually chase away the vultures.

# The Hunted

Animals use various strategies to avoid predators, which influence their behaviour, habitat choice and social habits. The leaf-eating browsers live in small family groups in dense thickets. This decreases the chances of a predator finding them. Their coat colour is usually broken by stripes or spots, helping to camouflage them amongst the leaves and branches. When approached by a predator they stand still to avoid being spotted. If they are threatened they scatter apart, making it difficult for predators to select a single animal.

The grass-eating grazers, on the other hand, form large groups that stampede when threatened by a predator. They depend on habitats with good visibility to be able to spot predators approaching from a distance.

## Giraffe ►

*Giraffa camelopardalis*: height: M: 4,9 - 5,2m; F: 4,3 - 4,6m; mass: M: 990 - 1 400kg, F: 700 - 970kg; life expectancy: 20 - 30 years.
From their height giraffe can spot a predator far off, and can move away fast when threatened. They defend themselves and their young by kicking the predator with their front legs. They are most vulnerable when bending low to drink water, or when crossing a slippery tar road.

## Thomson's Gazelle ▼

*Gazella thomsonii*: height: 70cm; mass: 14 - 16kg; life expectancy: 10 years. Along with widebeest and zebra, this is one of the major migrant species. They live in herds which vary from a few dozen up to about 1 000 whilst on migration. They are the main prey species for cheetah.

Predator - Lioness

## Buffalo ►

*Syncerus caffer*: height: 1,6m; mass: M: 800kg, F: 750kg; life expectancy: 15 - 20 years.
Buffalo are fairly safe from all predators including lions, because of both the size of individuals, and the number in the herd. A group of adults will chase away even a pride of lions. When buffalo do stampede they stick close together, making it difficult for individuals to be singled out and caught.

## ▲ Plains Zebra (Burchell's Zebra)

*Equus burchelli*: height: 1,3m; mass: 300 - 320kg; life expectancy: 20 years.
Both zebra and wildebeest congregate in large numbers on open plains. They are very alert, and often detect approaching predators in time to flee. The herds stampede in a large group, making it more difficult for individuals to be isolated and caught. Both wildebeest and zebra protect their infants when confronted by a single predator, but lone calves and foals are easy prey.

## White Bearded Gnu ►
## (Brindled Gnu/Blue Wildebeest)

*Connochaetes taurinus*: height: M 1,5m, F: 1,3m; mass: M 250kg, F: 180kg; life expectancy: 15-20 years

## ◄ Hippopotamus

*Hippopotamus amphibius*: height: 1,5m; mass: 1 500kg; life expectancy: 40 - 50 years.

## African Elephant ►

*Loxodonta africana*: height: 2,8m; mass: M: 5 750kg, F: 3 800kg; life expectancy: 55 - 60 years.

## ◄ Black Rhino (Hook-lipped)

*Diceros bicornis*: height: 1,6m; mass: 800 - 1 100kg; life expectancy: 30 - 40 years.

The adults of these three animals are too large for predators, even lion, to catch, and their only true enemy is humans. Lone calves of rhino, buffalo and elephant may be attacked by lions; lone hippo calves are sometimes attacked by crocodiles when the mother runs into the water.